UNDER MY
SKIN

ESSENTIAL POETS SERIES 212

Guernica Editions Inc. acknowledges the support of the Canada Council for the Arts and the Ontario Arts Council. The Ontario Arts Council is an agency of the Government of Ontario. We acknowledge the financial support of the Government of Canada through the National Translation Program for Book Publishing for our translation activities. We also acknowledge the financial support of the Government of Canada through the Canada Book Fund (CBF) for our publishing activities.

UNDER MY
SKIN

Orville Lloyd Douglas

GUERNICA

TORONTO – BUFFALO – LANCASTER (U.K.)

2014

Book design by Jamie Kerry of Belle Étoile Studios
www.belleetoilestudios.com

Kristin Gorsline, editor
Michael Mirolla, general editor
Guernica Editions Inc.
P.O. Box 76080, Abbey Market, Oakville,
(ON), Canada L6M 3H5
2250 Military Road, Tonawanda, N.Y. 14150-6000 U.S.A.

Distributors:
University of Toronto Press Distribution,
5201 Dufferin Street, Toronto (ON), Canada M3H 5T8
Gazelle Book Services, White Cross Mills,
High Town, Lancaster LA1 4XS U.K.

First edition.
Printed in Canada.

Legal Deposit – First Quarter

Library of Congress Catalog Card Number: 2013953842
**Library and Archives Canada
Cataloguing in Publication**
Douglas, Orville Lloyd, 1976-, author
Under my skin / Orville Lloyd Douglas.
(Essential poets series ; 212)
Poems.
Issued in print and electronic formats.
ISBN 978-1-55071-849-2 (pbk.).
ISBN 978-1-55071-850-8 (epub).
ISBN 978-1-55071-851-5 (mobi)
I. Title. II. Series: Essential poets series ; 212
PS8607.O93U53 2014   C811'.6
C2013-907544-5   C2013-907545-3

CONTENTS

I. Illusions of Canada

II. The Gospels

III. Dear Langston Hughes

IV. Vick

V. Wet Dreams

VI. Under the Skin

I

ILLUSIONS OF CANADA

Africville

Off the tip of Halifax, standing
At the edge of apartheid
On the ravaged coast
Was peace
Until Lester B. Pearson came

For decades the leaves bloomed and died here
Life thrived here
Wooden homes clean as a whistle
Lawns slick as the dew

Knowledge had a base here
An oral tradition
Like Zora's Eatonville

Hurston would have loved this place
Singing, dancing, hollering, hard working
Walking with her pen and paper
Recording joyous life

Skin of folks
It had a name
It had a game

It had a home
It had a soul

Blood, sweat, tears

Cleared, uprooted, shipped off
Bulldozed for a pittance
Less than a fucking grand

The revolution of 1812
Split mind like the Loyalists
Razor-sharp waves crashing

Flushing away all remnant of thought
To where they think blacks should be

Hell, you know, democracy is the Maple Leaf
Red and white
Yes, white, plain white

Yet this place had pride as thunderous as the Bay of
Fundy
A binding world of settlement, thought, expression
Civil rights fights here in the '60s every day

Yet the sewer system of red tape plowed through
Gouging out destruction
To what? For what?

Where were you?
Where was that motherfucker, Lester B.?
This wasn't Birmingham or Little Rock

No Scout, Mr. Finch or Harper Lee
No Jackson, Eldridge Cleaver, no Baldwin
No King, Kennedy, Nixon or Johnson

Where were we my brothers, my sisters
If blood is blood
And sweat is sweat?

They say snowflakes are daggers
And sickle blades struck the spirit of this abode

DISCOVER

READ

EXPLORE

LEARN

NEW HANOVER COUNTY PUBLIC LIBRARY

If found, please return to:
201 Chestnut St.
Wilmington, NC 28401
(910) 798-6300
http://www.nhclibrary.org

Orville Lloyd Douglas

UNDER MY
SKIN

GUERNICA EDITIONS

To some it's like a cemetery
Its gates once closed
Now a decrepit park

Soil once so rich you could eat it
Now buried six feet
But not forgotten

Alberta

In Edmonton, we are outnumbered for the hockey game
We are summoned to stand tall while the national anthem
Is blasted out of the loud speakers and children munch on
popcorn

Canada's national game is supposed to be a fun affair

The audience screams as youth-stealth bodies race across ice
Their sticks carve out territory
Space is precious just like land

The game is tied two apiece

There is only one Cree man and he is on the visiting team
He stands out like a sore thumb, skates fast like Sidney
Crosby
Gets the shit kicked out of him on the rink

He shoots, he scores!

The announcer's jubilant voice cries
The knockout goal gives the visitors their victory
The marauders spit on him

In this oil-drenched place to the west
Soaked with billions upon billions of surplus
No one moves

No Guardian Angel

Tonight at 11 p.m.
Walking to the run-down bus stop
Waiting as the heat cools into the night

I am bound to the sidewalk
Moving up and down, back and forth
Covering my bald head with my windbreaker

The neon-red lights sweep up to me
Floodlights of slavery shine in my face
The master barking at me like a dog

I don't recall it being 1842
Picking cotton isn't my occupation
Didn't see no Coloured Only signs on this block

My house is the house with the green lawn
– It's the home of hard work and sacrifice
It's the dream of immigrants –

Down that way, right by the group home
With the windows slammed shut
Where the other cruisers are situated

I laugh as he snickers and bellows
"I want some identification!"
He punches some numbers into the computer

Didn't know apartheid was Canada's new declaration
for his delight
Guess you got nothing better to do
Than catch some man in the bushes?

Not worried about the shootings at Bramalea
Or the rape at Yonge and Bloor
Or the gang wars in Scarborough

East York, Parkdale … I'm not Oprah
I can't solve race relations in an hour
No national stage to speak

My heart beats rapidly
He says, "You're free to go"
I am manumitted in this moment

I don't move, just stare into his dead-blue eyes
A snarling grin on his pale face
I want to smash his pupils with my fists

Wasting time …
My card has been processed
I can move on

Brother

A blond man with conviction
Decides to conquer the distance
He doesn't wait in the ditch
He doesn't stare with perplexed anguish

This Adonis knows what he wants, unlike you my brother

I have been told that I am not black enough
Not authentic because I am not down
Because I don't speak Jamaican patois
Don't hang out at the coolest hip-hop joints in Toronto

Listening to reggae and calypso with a Caribbean fla-
vour isn't my scene

But I am not a brother anymore, not part of the pack
Since all the brothers choose to ignore me
Because a pale hand is on my behind
A milky mouth against my manhood ...

I have no groove man?

Do I got to read Malcolm X to be like you?
Wear the African cloth
Speak about Nigeria, Botswana and Niger?

Are you the general ordering me around?
Or trying to be Lincoln?
This isn't the Emancipation Proclamation
We aren't in Dixie, man!

You speak to me with ferocious eyes
In the audience stand your followers
You speak Africa to me
Hell, you even bought the bookstore

So I got no soul anymore?
My tongue racing against the Caucasian next to me

But in the North, in the woods
You're fucking full of it
Pushing a lascivious mouth onto the head of Africa
The reflection of your crimes of passion knows no bounds

Come on, soul brother
My nigga, why do you care?
You going to lecture me?

Just move on nigga
Move on

Building the Black Penis

Every Black Man's got one
The colour is lascivious
When the faggots on Church Street see it
They want it with a hunger in their eyes
Salivating

Do you sit around all day dreaming about it?
Search Africa, Europe,
North America, the Caribbean for it
A commodity, a transaction
That doesn't have a name

They don't want to see a face

Are our dicks greater than the CN Tower?
Does the phallic symbol mean something to you?
Maybe it should be on a stage
Shaking its black ass for some dollars

Or on a DVD for your private screening
Behind closed corridors
Trapped in darkness

But not on the political forum
Not in print or plays or television
Never Managing Editor or Editor-in-Chief

Remember, it's just the Black Penis
Close your eyes
Feel the bitterness

Below the layers of denim
Underneath the sprawling wilderness of deceit
In the exotic jungle down there

Canada Is Shit

Whenever I take a shit, I think of Canada
Trying to expunge all the negativity out my hole
It's tough sometimes, I think I've got constipation
Newspapers littered with supremacy and lies
The aggravation lodged inside

Today, I'm rushing to the bathroom
Squat my black ass down
Nothing coming out
Take a deep gulp
Exhale
Irritation
Blasting it out in clumps
Brothers beat by the boys in blue
Toronto, Montreal, Halifax – take your pick
Three hundred and sixty-five days

At the bottom of the toilet is Canada
All the brainwashing from reading this lexicon
The crap about a unified nation
The rich prestige of diversity and the sewage of contempt
The façade that we are all Canadians in the Great White
North
Except I only see people that look like me on the six
o'clock news
Or plastered on the cover of daily papers
Brothers in handcuffs
Cockroaches, rodents and ants receive better treatment
than us

Grab the toilet paper
Wipe away the deleterious filth
Cleaning off all the self-hatred
The dangerousness of multiculturalism is not to be believed
O *Canada* is an anthem that ignores dark-skinned folks
like me
I won't pledge allegiance to your white Queen
When Toronto's mayor and police chief are always white
While black folks live in chains in Regent Park and Malvern

Saunter to the ceramic sink
Wash off the soap scum
The unsavory nature of this so-called nation
Open the window to let out the stench of hypocrisy
The rancid odour moving up and away

My ass is clean now, too bad Canada isn't

II

THE GOSPELS

Choir Boy

Lanky, tall, thin
Smooth, stupid, young
He capitulates to his master as the terror throbs in his soul

Wear the crisp white shirt and black trousers
Sing like a canary on Sunday
The parishioners love it

Shine those shoes until God can see the polish
Don't be nervous
He'll be gentle

I know the terror behind oak doors
Are you still sore? Be a good choir boy
The Lord wouldn't have it any other way

Origin of Species

Let this last forever
This unsavory touch
Let it burn like a cold sore
Fiery, blister, open wound

See it scorch as an inferno
Off the sunset
Not touching the clouds
Not feeling serenity

The second is never remembered like the first
Since one comes before two

This is the origin of species
An experience can only be new once
Not twice, not three, or four times
When you feel something you know it

No need to press the replay button
Start over
Two is the second fiddle
Disappearing behind the opaque clouds

One comes before two
Not the other way around
It is linear, not transparent
Not natural selection

Beautiful

You say I am so beautiful that I hate myself
I am so handsome that I want to slash my face with a razor
Twist the blade so crimson blood pours out my hollow vessel

Yes, I am so attractive that the ugliness within is my saviour
I am so beautiful, so shallow and superficial
So pretty my soul is filth

Confession

This moment is distinctive as a battered oyster shell
Round, breakable, insignificant
Striking in contrast with reality

Bathed in grey, as grey as the second you arrived
Glancing at your watch, wondering and wanting to flee

It will be brief

A man-child too timid and frivolous
Sitting on the stoop of the brownstone waiting

Waiting

Waiting

No need to say anything
And so we walked by this

The Terror Within Us

I committed a crime worthy of murder
I felt blackness deep inside of me

Our spirits twisted and turned as ecstasy erupted from
within us
A tongue travelled up my shivering spine and I cried
with desire
Our bodies intertwined as sweat poured down our faces
and backs
My fingers glided across a hairy chest, toned thighs and
midnight skin
Our chocolate lips ignited a fire that wasn't suffocated

We meet when night falls, in a brownstone
We can't walk down the street for fear of daggers
But in the dark, is a kiss not a kiss?
When our hearts pound against our conscience, is it
not love?

Golden Boy

You've got the golden touch
That old black magic

Illusion is your grandeur
Your halo

You are Moses
Man of the Mountain

Yet, unable to separate image from substance
Your last testament is hollow

The text is gibberish
Believe the words of Our Savior

The Lord is the master we pledge allegiance to
We pray at church every Sunday

But you are as vindictive as Caleb and Abel
You siphon our money away

Every week the ritual begins again
Losing ourselves to the millennia-year-old book

Twenty-Five

A quarter century of life never to be revisited
One thousand, three hundred weeks of existence

Gone are the bright lemon yellow crayons
Inside the window I see a depraved black boy

A man-child still playing foolish games
Struggling in a world that knows no limits

He draws in the few strands of happiness
With a brilliant saffron flourish

Brushing out paintings of remembrance
Erasing events charred with rage

The solitude is honesty, as is silence
The world is a sharp shade of black

It is concealed in a black box
It is me

Scarlet

The sky is a blazing scarlet as the rain poured blood out
of the faucet
Down, down, down, flooding the mind with doubt
The uneasiness stinging from a swarm of bees
The jagged edge you grasp in your fingers
Should you make the final cut?
Every disappointing moment builds another layer of pain
Make a large S into flesh
Yes, the sky is scarlet, so pernicious to stare at, yet so real

Perhaps

Perhaps it was better that you did?
Just don't be degrading and despicable

If you want to do it, please do it on your own time
Not during family hour or when guests are over

Look at our neighbourhood, I don't want gossiping
No whispering along the block

Mrs. Witherspoon is nosy
She knows all the stories behind the walls of suburbia

Please cover your tracks
We don't want Pandora's box to explode

You have your options, either use pills or some elixirs
Please, please, please, don't do it in the kitchen

We have company coming over
I don't want anything splattering on the good china

Everything must stay the same, as though time has not
passed
Remember, we just bought a new oak table for the
dining room

Just do it quickly, dig a shallow grave
Place some red tulips or roses over it

Don't write some note saying we caused this either
You brought it on yourself

You had everything, the best of the world

Still Standing

Let the gospel choir fill their lungs with glee
Let the eulogy commence

The flying hands in the air
The sobbing sounds of hundreds dressed in black
Kleenexes used to cast away salty tears

> *Never Again*
> *Never Again …*

It's the same marching song
Of never again
But this will happen again

Sweat pouring profusely down the brows
Of blue and white gowns
Trying to breathe between speaking in tongues

The classic mother grieving over her boy
She flung herself on to the coffin –
Why was she so surprised?

He hung out at the crack house on Jane and Finch
Twenty-eight, four kids, no job
He bought you the DVDs and television set with blood money

Don't act so surprised that I'm the black faggot
Alive, in the background

III

DEAR LANGSTON HUGHES

Dear Langston Hughes

Was it you at the Savoy the other day?
Talking to Alain Locke as I blurred in the smoke?
Sitting at the table, I wanted to be with you …
But you already know what I desire
Don't you, Langston?

Were we dancing on Lenox Avenue in a twirl
Shaking and moving to the *Charleston*
Last night I loved *Shuffle Along*
And Josephine was amazing!

Bessie sang her sorrowful tune for all to see
Gladys Bentley was just rocking at that piano –
She can really tickle the ivory, can't she?

Zora had a wonderful feast last night
I laughed so hard when she talked about "Godmother"
Why didn't you invite me on Zora's folklore trip
The one down South with Jesse?

All you talk about is Carl, Carl, Carl!
Yes, I read *Nigger Heaven* and I enjoyed it
Although W.E.B. Du Bois attacked him, Van Vechten
is not the enemy
After all, he helped you get that book deal –
Why the reticence, Langston?

When we were at that drag ball
You clapped and smiled as the queens moved by –
Shall I tell Harold Jackman and Countee Cullen you say
hello?

When the night falls, I feel your ebony hand
It caresses my spirit, it ignites a fire within me
You stand in front of me, even though
you are only five foot four holding me tight
I feel at peace with you

Waves of pleasure erupt as our bodies drenched with guilt
wake up
The sky is a desolate shade of blue
When we leave your apartment, you won't hold my hand
outside
No kisses, hugs or a caress of my face at the café

Yet as the phoenix arises, I don't hear from you for weeks
I wonder if I have done something wrong –
Langston, is your image more important than love?
Is illusion your truth?

You're definitely not like Bruce or Aaron
But you helped us get the booklet together
Too bad it burned in a fire

I can't go on like this, Langston
How is your mother, Mrs. Hughes, by the way?
I never did get that Thanksgiving turkey in Cleveland

Perfidious Dreams

If I was Chopin and you were Freud
Who would win my heart?

Is it too simple to just fall in love with someone
To trust another person and lose yourself?

Would you be the id, ego
      or superego?

Would your madness smash down on us
Like an avalanche of fear?

Crashing through that narcissistic arrogance
You sharpen like a sickle

I dream of being in Versailles
Yet all you see is your reflection shattering

Guess the King Louis fable suits you well
Should I clap at the West End while you wax on about
tautology?

Voltaire is shrewd, but not you my dear
Are you the man in Trafalgar Square acting so –
      pulchritudinous?

It's Hamlet all over again in Copenhagen
Trapped in that frigging kingdom
Laertes won't save me

You believe I am diaphanous, but that's you
I'm not going down like Ophelia

You can be the one submerging in that muddy water of
sorrow

I won't be Lady Macbeth either
Don't pretend to be Iago, I beat you to it

Claudius and Robin Hood will be galloping away
With me from you

Surrender

Does the heavy heart surrender if the beat is weak
And the spirit once a sunburst is now just a flicker?
No job, no future, despite a university education
Your qualifications are just as good as pale-skinned folks

Should dreams fade when reality sets in?
Black skin, black mind, white masks the marathon of life
The walls of truth cause doubt, there is no way out

Is swallowing pills the ultimate conclusion
to the mind's peripatetic juncture?

Hope strangles happiness and squeezes life into a pulp
What if a bleeding wrist is the right resolution?
To be black and male and to pray to God for a peace
that never arrives
Why fight for life? Is it really surrendered?

Maybe or maybe not

IV

VICK

The Love Object

I have placed you on a shrine

Diligently polishing, perfecting

A platform of hallucinations

For hours staring at you

Wishing, wondering, if this devotion will become love

On a throne of delusions and grandeur

I imagine you to be magnanimous

And try to make myself palatable

Vick

Every man that I have ever known has wanted just one thing
But you are different
You desire to peek into my soul and see the real me
A me that I have been terrified to expose
Your skin is a light caramel brown
Your scent is cinnamon
Your words are like a sanctuary
A sacred place that makes me all effervescent inside

Your smile is irresistible like a papaya drink
Your eyes have clarity of optimism and youth
You are filled with passion, pathos and mystery
Your heart is the size of India
Your generosity knows no boundaries

You steer me right when I've withdrawn off course
You are not an Olympic athlete
But you have the valour of a champion
Your name is Vikas but you prefer to be called Vick
How I love thee

When you speak
You have hope
How I hope you never lose your infectious spirit and pride
How I wish you eternal happiness

Who is the real Vick?
I want to peel beyond the surface
Unleash the truth
Is he the passive-aggressive man?
The one with the sad sulk and pout?

Speak to me
Lecture me
Absolve me
How I love thee

Touch Me

Touch me, but not with your hands
Soothe me with kindness and generosity
Hold me in your memories so your spirit caresses the doubt
Move me with your empathy
Speak to me, but not with words
See me with your heart
Believe me, I do love you

Worth?

The eclipse is an omen, some believe
A primal signal of eternity

The burning orange ring in the sky
Exploded over the brownstone

Engulfing the rustic sheets, submerging tongues
Diving and somersaults
Over and over

Hair, wet hair, twisting and turning
Assiduously taking time through these thighs
Underneath crevices, below,
Over ankles, knees

Pounding your way through my buttocks
Bent over, you tell me you love me

A phone ringing in the distance
Only a couple of minutes
But we didn't care

A twist of flesh, the swift movement of a touch
The books fell off the dresser
What is it worth?

The elegance

Sweet

Elegance of it

That tender moment
To feel alive, to breathe in
What was that worth to be a problem?

Passion

It only takes one glance, one moment, one second, to reminisce
All I have to do is imagine with my eyes wide open
Your manhood is more potent than a drug
I trembled when your warm hands touched my soft skin and surrendered
The euphoria was overwhelming
When you exploded, you screamed in Punjabi
I swallowed the warm honey and savoured it
Your tongue travelled from the fire in Mumbai
Was drenched in the sweltering heat of Kingston, Jamaica
Then across the universe of solitude in Markham, Ontario, to me
For a long time I didn't know this love was deleterious
I'd close my eyes, praying it was an illusion
I had this dream that we'd wake up in bed on a Sunday morning with tea and coffee brewing
I can smell the roti, mango lassi, ackee and saltfish, dumplings and samosas
We were reading the *Toronto Star* together, celebrating our eighth anniversary
You promised me we would visit India soon
I still hold on to that, hoping it will happen
Then tears streamed down your face
You said you were crying about your dog, Jimmy
He died when you were six years old, but that was a long time ago, in the Punjab
I kissed you and we embraced
I wanted to lie to you and say everything was going to be alright
The stack of gifts, the well-wishes, the ceremonial mixture of East and West

You said this was not God's way
But you are not a Christian; you are Sikh
Two men loving each other should not be shameful in
any faith
That incident was a year ago.
I fall asleep now, awaking suddenly, feeling inadequate
and ignorant
Jump out of bed, search the house, but you are not here
I remember walking in Markham
I saw you holding a newborn and enjoying a picnic
with your beloved
Your folks had smiles on their faces, but you were solemn
The bitterness ate at my heart
I cringed when you kissed your wife and your mother smiled
Her womb was full again from your husbandly duty
I wanted to pull her hair out
Instead, I stood in the shadows, lurking, seething with desire
The camera clicking, your baby crying for breast milk
I turned away from your family moment
I guess it was easy for you to decide
I understand: sometimes passion isn't enough

One

Just one touch in the dark
One taste of apathy
One smoke of grief

One simple embrace
One feeling of a beat
Rumbling, shaking, shoving

Pushing, hustling, running
Gasping, wheezing, peeling
You wanted just one

Just one
Just one
Just one

And yet
Where are you?

This illusion of romance is killing me
I would rather my last breath on this planet be of some-
thing else
One omen of truth that we can survive this pain

This fable is not a novel I can discern fact from fiction
Turn the page of our destiny
One more day thinking about us is not worth it

Common Ground

It was either passion or purgatory
Ecstasy or rage
Blood or tears
We were on opposite continents
The violence of your seismic outbursts
Like an alcoholic in a drunken stupor
Your rage was irrational
Yet there was something peculiar and opaque
Something hidden, something distant
Too foreign
You spoke another language
You talked about your culture
You were trying to flee your demons
Your secrets, your guilt, your being the only son
I wanted to give you my life jacket
I dreamed there was something tangible to hold us
together
You tried cold turkey to stop drinking
You smoked your life away
Choked on your pain
Vomited from the disgust of your reflection

The Saddest Day Of Our Lives

It was a Friday evening in late September
We stood by the bus stop
This was not reconciliation or an apology
It was undisguised acceptance
You could remain a prisoner but I was cognizant
That being locked in a closet is not happiness

A little bit past 11 p.m. you let loose your irrational
venom
It pierced my skin, a ten-inch blade aimed at my heart
I tried to remain composed
Stumbled through rage, contempt – feeling
somnambulistic
There are three sides to every fable
Sometimes, no matter how much we want something
It just wasn't meant to be

Photographs From Markham, Ontario

In this photograph, we are standing on Centre Island
Your arms are wrapped around me
You softly say you love me
I feel your hairy brown face against my ebony skin
I want to believe this is real love
You press your teeth against my throat like a grizzly bear
Being subtle was never your strength
Our eyes are burning like a smoldering fire
A passion explodes from our glances

In the next picture, your fingers playfully caress my groin
The waves of Lake Ontario are on the horizon
I want to hold on to this moment forever and lock it in
a vault
To hold on to these feelings that thrives in my memories
But as I stare closer the residue is ash
A reflection of you with bloodshot eyes peers out
I cringe remembering how you told me you spent three
hundred dollars
From every pay cheque "purchasing happiness"
Your comatose look is prescient
You thought contentment was smoking away your future

In another photograph, I taste the rum
Wine and weed from your mouth on my lips
You hold a vodka bottle in your hand
You look like a hobo walking down Yonge Street

Then a series of shots with you vomiting on the cement
I stand motionless behind you, eyes wide
Splashes of flashbulbs are visible as the ambulance arrives
You screamed that your parents might find out the truth

The police report would indicate you were intoxicated
Your immaturity clouded your judgment

There are no photographs from the hospital
Where I watched you slumber, seething with disgust at
5 a.m.
Wrapped in blankets, your body living in some winter
wonderland
The nurse lecturing me on how the intravenous tubes
must flow into your system
That Sunday morning, standing over your weak body
I wanted to take the pillow from your cot and smother you
I prayed to Jesus Christ to kill you in your sleep
So I could go home instead of babysitting you

Today, I place the album in the garbage bin and light a match
I watch the flames extinguish your existence

V

WET DREAMS

Holy Dream

If I sucked God's thick ten-inch cock am I a sinner?
When I fucked Judas up his hairy ass did he cum?
I won't be punished for being myself

Does Jesus Christ like to get screwed on Sunday?
Tasting the sweet nectar of the essence of man

I love sucking dick
And I like getting a real nice blow job
The feeling of another man giving me pleasure

I won't feel guilty
I deserve to be loved

I am bones, particles, atoms
Lies, secrets, depression, reality

I am not a pastor
Nor am I his sweet wife that is silent
I do not live in that cult of the so-called family

I am a sinner

I will be the outcast
I am me

Temple

Every night
I pray to this majestic
Mystical

Thick
Hard
Deity

I am travelling
Discovering
up
up
Up

This steep mountain

It's a temple of fire
Molten lava explodes
It's
A fucking

Eruption!

Don't want to
Disrupt this
Sleeping
Giant

The hand and a finger
Across rough terrain

Fingers
Prodding
Moving
Your body begins to shake like an earthquake

Your love explodes across my chest

As your milk covers my face

Memories

to Edward

Rape me with your tongue
Abuse me, your manly hands crushing my bones
Seduce me as the heart wavers

Torture me because
The ferocious hurricane of passion
Causes me to me bleed, surrender

Ripping apart my sanctuary
Spread eagle on the mattress
On top, you are the man in control

Tell me about Accra
Of the magnificent skyscrapers
Speak to me of the spirit of Ghana

Remind me Africa isn't just the jungle
It's a voyage, these hands
Moving across this dark body

Up and back, through thunderous thighs
Over to Pretoria, to the Cape of Good Hope
Ready to mount me with your gigantic cock

Show me with your lips the power of the African man
Oh, they're black, yes, jet black

Push harder, press down firm against my ass
Unraveling the stories, the fables you told –
The postcard from Durban was extraordinary …

Mombasa … What a dream …
Dancing on that beach …
I want to go on a safari with you

Pound your way through the lies we keep
Read me one of your surreptitious poems
Plunder your way to Nairobi and over to Harare …

Cranking out each emotion
I engulf my way down
Pressing your penis to the back of my throat

All the way back, the eyes watering
Holding in your love
Now you feign being asleep

Roll over, reason with me
Plead with me
Awake me with your manhood

Call those ten digits
Again
Let me hold on to these memories

Crimes Of Passion

I sucked your husband's cock on your leather sofa last night
I was on my hands and knees engulfing his thick and
firm eight inches
I spread your spouse's cheeks on the coffee table
Pounded him by your shrine of photos
Smashing your wedding-day pictures
The twin silver frames crashing to the floor
The fragments of your marriage no longer a riddle to solve

I fucked your man doggy style on your matrimonial bed
My stiff cock hard inside his ass
Punishing him for our sinful act of revenge
His eyes refusing to look at me
We both love the same man but only one of us can win

Rolling over after, he kissed me gently on the lips
His mouth sour, filled with acid and bleach
I could've killed him with my bare hands
Strangled his throat full of false promises and concessions
Crushed his skull with my fists one million times

I jumped up and put my clothes on
Glanced at the photographs in the hallway
You in your wedding gown and your son's tenth birth-
day party
I never looked back

Slut

The slut is an endangered species
An enigma of our fears and dreams

The slut is not a whore

The slut lurks in our fantasies and our nightmares
Sucking the cocks of boyfriends and husbands in
expensive suits and ties

The slut has the ambition, drive, and nerve to succeed
To go after whomever he or she desires

The slut understands there is no such thing as failure
Sex is not about gratification
It is about conquest fulfilling a prophecy

The slut is a warrior that fights
The slut lives and thrives within all of us

VI

UNDER THE SKIN

Another Language

If you look at the snow, you will notice
it speaks another language

You are cognizant at the checkout counter
that the signs you don't understand are in Swiss,
German, French, Italian

As you stand at the bus stop in Geneva,
Zurich, or Bern, the cold winter blast
freezes your invitation

Rain spits on your face, the texture of this
"wetness" the same as on the pale faces beside you

No need to translate the crinkling of noses,
sighs from lips, the blanket expressions.

No need to be Jacques Cousteau and
travel to the depths of the Atlantic Ocean
to know the truth

No dictionary is necessary
The language test is a constellation
of hearts as hard as stone

It is the lexicon of disgrace

Typically Black

In this town there are hundreds of Tanya's
Just fifteen, pushing run-down strollers
Talking on their cell phones
Buying Pampers and formula

The ring is no issue here
Tanya's mama Joyce was full-womb herself
Thirty-eight, with Tanya inside
And a large brood at home

She is a modern welfare queen
Never dreamed beyond Jane and Finch
Getting a bachelor's isn't in her imagination
Her goal is living it to tomorrow

The demise is psychic
She's behind in rent
Baby-daddy gone
They'll be evicted Monday

There is no such thing as luck
Reconstruction didn't build new dwellings
What was that plan back in the '60s:
Immigration + Jobs = Prosperous Canada?

At the supermarket, Jamal tries to steal a candy
Never mind he's two-years-old
Jamal's mother's hand smacks him against his back
The pain is like hot fire,
It hits an emotional chord like the Randal Dooley case

The boy bawls in aisle three
Screeching and clawing by the sugar and sweets
Yet this termagant is safeguarded
The whole store immobile

Mama blasts Jamal at her tirade again
Slaps Jamal across the face, "dumb like your father"
Then begins to pray for his soul
As if religion is going to save a child from this terror

The second is a prism
The commotion ripples comments through the store –
Should someone summon the strength?
Or is it because of colour?

Jamal is strangled out of the store
The barrier remains erect

One Million Dollars

You prowl on the stage like a panther in heat
Spreading the message from Montreal to Vancouver
The white lights flood your ego
This is your halo

You are a Canadian idol
The stage is your temple where you are loved by millions
In a trance, they see your diamonds
Your flash

You are Jesus Christ of Nazareth
This resurrection on to Jericho, then Israel
You wear the shiny medallion they shot James for
The Nikes that Delroy beat the shit out of Andy for

You make them spend their hard-earned cash on concert
tickets
Albums and DVDs
Your words are scripture
The masses are nailed to the cross
Their blood, their deaths, their lives spin you gold

Dwayne raped Tamika – she was only fourteen
Her pussy was so young – but you don't care
After all, eating out young girls is what an artist brags about
And he's *your* bodyguard

Tamika just wanted an autograph
Dwayne told her how to get it
Then forced himself through
Tamika screaming so loud that no one heard

He's your brother
He's your father
He's your grandfather

Your people tell you this is a charity event
They've got the envelope of your entitlement
Ten minutes for the masses
Then back to your mansion in Rosedale

You Know Everything

Run DMC and Public Enemy are out
50 Cent and Kanye West are in
Yeah, you're really black
You've read *The Color Purple* and *Black Like Me* one million
times
But your skin colour is neutral, it doesn't define or bind you
Yeah, you're really black
You quote Angela Davis and Frantz Fanon like scripture
Reading academic books don't provide the complete picture
Martin Luther King is your Emancipation Proclamation
Ignoring your privilege is a form of indoctrination
So, I'm your friend now, why?
Would you trade places with Trayvon Martin
Walk the wrong neighbourhood and die?
You know what it's like on the subway or the bus
People standing clear or inching away, making a fuss
An old white lady clutching her purse
Being different is like a curse
Yeah, you're really black
You are so *down* my brother
But you don't want to live in my section of town

The Perception

Shattered glass is always the way to the truth
Shaking, vomiting, confusion
Past the first trimester

It was the detour he didn't want
From his promising NFL career
He has a decision to make have a ceremony or living in sin

The message sent through in the middle of the night
A forced entry he wasn't there to stop
With unfinished results

Driving to his house, thinking of an explanation
He wanted termination
But it's the woman's choice

The sports harem is only for the "chosen"
She didn't listen. Now she's considered licentious
He's no longer the perfect brand

White Guilt

You gain pleasure from charging into the bath houses

On the weekends

You're searching, prowling down the corridors

For some chocolate popsicles

Or maybe you want to taste some Mexican or Thai?

You've studied post-colonial literature, George Elliott
Clarke and Dionne Brand

You dated someone of a different shade

When you were in college

You're immune to having dark thoughts

On your birthday, your daughter announces
she's marrying an Asian man
He may be smart, nice, dependable
He might be sweet, attractive, have a great sense of humour

Yet he just wouldn't look right in family portraits
The ones you send to relatives in San Diego, Zurich
and Berlin
You don't want your daughter to know you agree

So you smile and continue the façade
He's a nice chap, you think
Slice open the flesh of the meat

Carve your disgust into the chicken
Chewing harder into the green pepper
Drinking the wine as though it was oil

You give a bittersweet smile as you think
How you could strangle your daughter's new fiancé
Dig a shallow grave in the backyard

New neighbours have moved in on your street
You see them in the kitchen, baking pie
Their skin is awfully tan

But you smile again, decide to say hello anyway
After all, you're such a nice person
And everybody has these kinds of thoughts

I Kissed Adolf Hitler On The Lips

I returned to Deutschland and kissed Adolf Hitler right on the lips
We are connected through misery
Adolf told me he needed more living space, that's why he expanded
Gave me a tour of his camps and ovens
We drank crimson wine on our a trip down the Rhine

I told him we're working on our own in the Great White North
Pale-faced folks are screaming no more government handouts
Feces, dirty water, shoddy housing are our gifts to the First Nation's people
Five hundred Aboriginal women's ghosts haunt our lives
Parts of Canada are paradise, while others resemble third world nations

Everyone has amnesia, forgets the sacred document of 1876
Divide and conquer was the strategy that destroyed the lives of our fellow citizens
United Nations' soldiers aren't setting up in Winnipeg, Vancouver or Toronto
Red Cross and World Vision plead for money to save the dying Africans
Yet our own people are living in disgrace

The Rage Within Me

It is bubbling beneath the surface
This discontent
Irritation like a cancer that has no cure
The blood is boiling
Illogical comments, statements
More violent than bones being crushed in a train wreck
Mangled spirits and destroyed dreams
Ignorance is the way this game is played
I won't wait another moment to be politically correct
My thoughts will be a sledgehammer to smash the doc-
trine of my oppressors
I would murder millions if my words could kill

ABOUT THE AUTHOR

Orville Lloyd Douglas is a writer and social activist. His writing examines image versus reality of tolerance and multiculturalism in Canada from the perspective of a young, gay, black man. His poetry has been published in various literary journals and anthologies across Canada; and his journalism has appeared in publications such as the *Toronto Star*, *Xtra*, *Word Magazine*, *Colorlines*, *Amöi*, and the *Guardian*. His poetry has received critical acclaim from George Elliott Clarke, who described Douglas' first collection, *You Don't Know Me* (TSAR, 2005), as "bold and brash," and Ginsbergesque in "the same pell-mell rush of ideas and images that drives *Howl*." Douglas resides in Brampton, Ontario.

mL

8-14